The Hagopian Institute, LLC has compiled the _Quote Junkie_ series. The overall series includes over 8,000 quotes, focusing mostly on short quotes that can be used in everyday life as sources of wisdom and inspiration. This particular edition of the series includes hilarious quotes by some of the most serious men and women ever to live on this planet. Please enjoy this edition of the series, and share these quotes with your coworkers, friends, and family.

Todd Hagopian

President

The Hagopian Institute, LLC

I0455404

A woman is the only thing I am afraid of that I know will not hurt me.

Abraham Lincoln

Better to remain silent and be thought a fool than to speak out and remove all doubt.

Abraham Lincoln

Common looking people are the best in the world: that is the reason the Lord makes so many of them.

Abraham Lincoln

Every one desires to live long, but no one would be old.

Abraham Lincoln

How many legs does a dog have if you call the tail a leg? Four. Calling a tail a leg doesn't make it a leg.

Abraham Lincoln

I can make more generals, but horses cost money.

Abraham Lincoln

If I were two-faced, would I be wearing this one?

Abraham Lincoln

If this is coffee, please bring me some tea; but if this is tea, please bring me some coffee.

Abraham Lincoln

Marriage is neither heaven nor hell, it is simply purgatory.

Abraham Lincoln

No man has a good enough memory to be a successful liar.

Abraham Lincoln

No matter how much cats fight, there always seem to be plenty of kittens.

Abraham Lincoln

Tact is the ability to describe others as they see themselves.

Abraham Lincoln

The best way to get a bad law repealed is to enforce it strictly.

Abraham Lincoln

The time comes upon every public man when it is best for him to keep his lips closed.

Abraham Lincoln

These capitalists generally act harmoniously and in concert, to fleece the people

Abraham Lincoln

What kills a skunk is the publicity it gives itself.

Abraham Lincoln

When you have got an elephant by the hind legs and he is trying to run away, it's best to let him run.

Abraham Lincoln

Whenever I hear anyone arguing for slavery, I feel a strong impulse to see it tried on him personally.

Abraham Lincoln

You have to do your own growing no matter how tall your grandfather was.

Abraham Lincoln

Man is a reasoning rather than a reasonable animal.

Alexander Hamilton

A well adjusted person is one who makes the same mistake twice without getting nervous.

Alexander Hamilton

I am dying from the treatment of too many physicians.

Alexander The Great

Liars need to have good memories.

Algernon Sydney

Well I just figure any man who risks his neck to save a dog's life isn't going to kill someone for gold teeth.

Alvin Adams

It is little men know of women; their smiles and their tears alike are seldom what they seem.

Amelia Barr

Old age is the verdict of life.

Amelia Barr

When men make themselves into brutes it is just to treat them like brutes.

Amelia Barr

Men would live exceedingly quiet if these two words, mine and thine, were taken away.

Anaxagoras

Every act you have ever performed since the day you were born was performed because you wanted something.

Andrew Carnegie

Fear not, the people may be deluded for a moment, but cannot be corrupted.

Andrew Jackson

It is a damn poor mind indeed which can't think of at least two ways to spell any word.

Andrew Jackson

There is no pleasure in having nothing to do; the fun is having lots to do and not doing it.

Andrew Jackson

Think of submitting our measure to the advice of politicians! I would as soon submit the subject of the equality of a goose to a fox.

Anna Howard Shaw

But he that dares not grasp the thorn Should never crave the rose.

Anne Bronte

I see that a man cannot give himself up to drinking without being miserable one-half his days and mad the other.

Anne Bronte

There is always a "but" in this imperfect world.

Anne Bronte

Personal beauty is a greater recommendation than any letter of reference.

Aristotle

The young are permanently in a state resembling intoxication.

Aristotle

Is boredom anything less than the sense of one's faculties slowly dying?

Arthur Schopenhauer

We all admire the wisdom of people who come to us for advice.

Arthur Schopenhauer

Will minus intellect constitutes vulgarity.

Arthur Schopenhauer

Wealth is like sea-water; the more we drink, the thirstier we become; and the same is true of fame.

Arthur Schopenhauer

We forfeit three-quarters of ourselves in order to be like other people.

Arthur Schopenhauer

The more unintelligent a man is, the less mysterious existence seems to him.

Arthur Schopenhauer

Just remember, once you're over the hill you begin to pick up speed.

Arthur Schopenhauer

Journalists are like dogs, when ever anything moves they begin to bark.

Arthur Schopenhauer

When one turns over in bed, it is time to turn out.

Arthur Wellesley

The whole art of war consists of guessing at what is on the other side of the hill.

Arthur Wellesley

The only thing I am afraid of is fear.

Arthur Wellesley

I don't know what effect these men will have upon the enemy, but, by God, they frighten me.

Arthur Wellesley

Being born in a stable does not make one a horse.

Arthur Wellesley

When one turns over in bed, it is time to turn out.

Arthur Wellesley

The whole art of war consists of guessing at what is on the other side of the hill.

Arthur Wellesley

The only thing I am afraid of is fear.

Arthur Wellesley

I don't know what effect these men will have upon the enemy, but, by God, they frighten me.

Arthur Wellesley

Being born in a stable does not make one a horse.

Arthur Wellesley

Hasten slowly

Augustus

A beautiful woman should break her mirror early.

Baltasar Gracian

Advice is sometimes transmitted more successfully through a joke than grave teaching.

Baltasar Gracian

Don't take the wrong side of an argument just because your opponent has taken the right side.

Baltasar Gracian

Dreams will get you nowhere, a good kick in the pants will take you a long way.

Baltasar Gracian

The things we remember best are those better forgotten.

Baltasar Gracian

If you don't enter the tiger's den, how can you catch the tiger's cub?

Ban Chao

An author is a fool who, not content with boring those he lives with, insists on boring future generations.

Baron de Montesquieu

I have always observed that to succeed in the world one should seem a fool, but be wise.

Baron de Montesquieu

The reason the Romans built their great paved highways was because they had such inconvenient footwear.

Baron de Montesquieu

What orators lack in depth they make up for in length.

Baron de Montesquieu

Bore: one who has the power of speech but not the capacity for conversation

Benjamin Disraeli

How much easier it is to be critical than to be correct.

Benjamin Disraeli

Little things affect little minds.

Benjamin Disraeli

Wine is constant proof that God loves us and loves to see us happy.

Benjamin Franklin

We are all born ignorant, but one must work hard to remain stupid.

Benjamin Franklin

To lengthen thy life, lessen thy meals.

Benjamin Franklin

Three can keep a secret, if two of them are dead.

Benjamin Franklin

There are three faithful friends - an old wife, an old dog, and ready money.

Benjamin Franklin

The worst wheel of the cart makes the most noise.

Benjamin Franklin

The U. S. Constitution doesn't guarantee happiness, only the pursuit of it. You have to catch up with it yourself.

Benjamin Franklin

The definition of insanity is doing the same thing over and over and expecting different results.

Benjamin Franklin

Some people die at 25 and aren't buried until 75.

Benjamin Franklin

Rather go to bed with out dinner than to rise in debt

Benjamin Franklin

Many foxes grow gray but few grow good.

Benjamin Franklin

Keep your eyes wide open before marriage, half shut afterwards.

Benjamin Franklin

In this world nothing is certain but death and taxes.

Benjamin Franklin

If you know how to spend less than you get, you have the philosopher's stone.

Benjamin Franklin

If a man could have half of his wishes, he would double his troubles.

Benjamin Franklin

I wake up every morning at nine and grab for the morning paper. Then I look at the obituary page. If my name is not on it, I get up.

Benjamin Franklin

I guess I don't so much mind being old, as I mind being fat and old.

Benjamin Franklin

I didn't fail the test, I just found 100 ways to do it wrong.

Benjamin Franklin

He who falls in love with himself will have no rivals.

Benjamin Franklin

He that speaks much, is much mistaken.

Benjamin Franklin

Half a truth is often a great lie.

Benjamin Franklin

Guests, like fish, begin to smell after three days.

Benjamin Franklin

Fatigue is the best pillow.

Benjamin Franklin

Beware of little expenses. A small leak will sink a great ship.

Benjamin Franklin

Beer is living proof that God loves us and wants us to be happy.

Benjamin Franklin

A man wrapped up in himself makes a very small bundle.

Benjamin Franklin

A learned blockhead is a greater blockhead than an ignorant one.

Benjamin Franklin

A countryman between two lawyers is like a fish between two cats.

Benjamin Franklin

At 20 years of age the will reigns; at 30 the wit; and at 40 the judgment.

Benjamin Franklin

He that is of the opinion money will do everything may well be suspected of doing everything for money.

Benjamin Franklin

To lengthen thy life, lessen thy meals.

Benjamin Franklin

A man wrapped up in himself makes a very small bundle.

Benjamin Franklin

A slip of the foot you may soon recover, but a slip of the tongue you may never get over.

Benjamin Franklin

The longest sword, the strongest lungs, the most voices, are false measures of truth.

Benjamin Whichcote

None are so empty as those who are full of themselves.

Benjamin Whichcote

We seldom call anybody lazy, but such as we reckon inferior to us, and of whom we expect some service.

Bernard Madeville

All human evil comes from a single cause, man's inability to sit still in a room.

Blaise Pascal

Few friendships would survive if each one knew what his friend says of him behind his back.

Blaise Pascal

I have made this letter longer than usual, only because I have not had the time to make it shorter.

Blaise Pascal

If all men knew what others say of them, there would not be four friends in the world.

Blaise Pascal

Too much and too little wine. Give him none, he cannot find truth; give him too much, the same.

Blaise Pascal

We only consult the ear because the heart is wanting.

Blaise Pascal

Any young man who is unmarried at the age of twenty one is a menace to the community.

Brigham Young

It is wise for us to forget our troubles, there are always new ones to replace them.

Brigham Young

Remember, a chip on the shoulder is a sure sign of wood higher up.

Brigham Young

Dog is not considered a good dog because he is a good barker. A man is not considered a good man because he is a good talker.

Buddha

Ennui has made more gamblers than avarice, more drunkards than thirst, and perhaps as many suicides as despair.

Buddha

Holding on to anger is like grasping a hot coal with the intent of throwing it at someone else; you are the one who gets burned.

Buddha

I do not believe in a fate that falls on men however they act; but I do believe in a fate that falls on them unless they act.

Buddha

The tongue like a sharp knife... Kills without drawing blood.

Buddha

If you don't say anything, you won't be called on to repeat it.

Calvin Coolidge

If Russians knew how to read, they would write me off.

Catherine The Great

I shall be an autocrat, that's my trade; and the good Lord will forgive me, that's his.

Catherine The Great

When I hear of an 'equity' in a case like this, I am reminded of a blind man in a dark room - looking for a black hat - which isn't there.

Charles Bowen

The rule in carving holds good as to criticism; never cut with a knife what you can cut with a spoon.

Charles Buxton

Credit is a system whereby a person who can not pay gets another person who can not pay to guarantee that he can pay.

Charles Dickens

Charity begins at home, and justice begins next door.

Charles Dickens

Credit is a system whereby a person who can't pay gets another person who can't pay to guarantee that he can pay.

Charles Dickens

He would make a lovely corpse.

Charles Dickens

If there were no bad people, there would be no good lawyers.

Charles Dickens

Regrets are the natural property of grey hairs.

Charles Dickens

There are books of which the backs and covers are by far the best parts.

Charles Dickens

There are only two styles of portrait painting; the serious and the smirk.

Charles Dickens

Vices are sometimes only virtues carried to excess!

Charles Dickens

We forge the chains we wear in life.

Charles Dickens

You don't carry in your countenance a letter of recommendation.

Charles Dickens

I am not disposed to complain that I have planted and others have gathered the fruits.

Charles Goodyear

Make 'em laugh; make 'em cry; make 'em wait.

Charles Reade

A ruffled mind makes a restless pillow.

Charlotte Bronte

Give him enough rope and he will hang himself.

Charlotte Bronte

I feel monotony and death to be almost the same.

Charlotte Bronte

Let your performance do the thinking.

Charlotte Bronte

Life is so constructed, that the event does not, cannot, will not, match the expectation.

Charlotte Bronte

Look twice before you leap.

Charlotte Bronte

There is only one difference between a madman and me. I am not mad.

Charlotte Bronte

I may be president of the United States, but my private life is nobody's damned business.

Chester Arthur

Mediocre men often have the most acquired knowledge.

Claude Bernard

It is what we know already that often prevents us from learning.

Claude Bernard

Acquaintance lessens fame.

Claudius

No one is more miserable than the person who wills everything and can do nothing.

Claudius

Say not always what you know, but always know what you say

Claudius

Fool! Don't you see now that I could have poisoned you a hundred times had I been able to live without you.

Cleopatra

He who learns but does not think, is lost! He who thinks but does not learn is in great danger.

Confucius

Never give a sword to a man who can't dance.

Confucius

Only the wisest and stupidest of men never change.

Confucius

To be wronged is nothing unless you continue to remember it.

Confucius

If I had learned education I would not have had time to learn anything else.

Cornelius Vanderbilt

What do I care about law? Ain't I got the power?

Cornelius Vanderbilt

You have undertaken to cheat me. I won't sue you, for the law is too slow. I will ruin you.

Cornelius Vanderbilt

In a cruel and evil world, being cynical can allow you to get some entertainment out of it.

Daniel Waters

A purpose, an intention, a design, strikes everywhere even the careless, the most stupid thinker.

David Hume

Generally speaking, the errors in religion are dangerous; those in philosophy only ridiculous.

David Hume

What a peculiar privilege has this little agitation of the brain which we call 'thought'.

David Hume

Business is other people's money.

Delphine de Girardin

Instinct is the nose of the mind.

Delphine de Girardin

Proof that they do not understand the republic is that in their fine promises for universal suffrage, they forgot women.

Delphine de Girardin

I would rather discover a single causal connection than win the throne of Persia.

Democritus

A good portion of speaking will consist in knowing how to lie.

Desiderius Erasmus

Fools are without number.

Desiderius Erasmus

In the kingdom of the blind, the one-eyed man is king.

Desiderius Erasmus

Man's mind is so formed that it is far more susceptible to falsehood than to truth.

Desiderius Erasmus

Women, can't live with them, can't live without them.

Desiderius Erasmus

Dogs and philosophers do the greatest good and get the fewest rewards.

Diogenes

I do not know whether there are gods, but there ought to be.

Diogenes

Man is the most intelligent of the animals - and the most silly.

Diogenes

We have two ears and one tongue so that we would listen more and talk less.

Diogenes

What I like to drink most is wine that belongs to others.

Diogenes

Why not whip the teacher when the pupil misbehaves?

Diogenes of Sinope

Of what use is a philosopher who doesn't hurt anybody's feelings?

Diogenes of Sinope

It is one of my sources of happiness never to desire a knowledge of other people's business.

Dolly Madison

His letter was like the shock produced by a cold bath.

Duff Green

Marriage, in life, is like a duel in the midst of a battle.

Edmund About

I never make the mistake of arguing with people for whose opinions I have no respect.

Edward Gibbon

Do not take life too seriously. You will never get out of it alive.

Elbert Hubbard

If you suffer, thank God! It is a sure sign that you are alive.

Elbert Hubbard

The world is moving so fast these days that the man who says it can't be done is generally interrupted by someone doing it.

Elbert Hubbard

You really couldn't be the same anymore than you could put the dress you were wearing back on the shelf in the store.

Eleanor Porter

Imparting knowledge is only lighting other men's candles at our lamp without depriving ourselves of any flame.

Eleanor Porter

As to Bell's talking telegraph, it only creates interest in scientific circles... its commercial values will be limited.

Elisha Gray

The cloud never comes from the quarter of the horizon from which we watch for it.

Elizabeth Gaskell

How easy it is to judge rightly after one sees what evil comes from judging wrongly!

Elizabeth Gaskell

I'll not listen to reason... reason always means what someone else has got to say.

Elizabeth Gaskell

Sometimes one likes foolish people for their folly, better than wise people for their wisdom.

Elizabeth Gaskell

Do not tell secrets to those whose faith and silence you have not already tested.

Elizabeth I

The stone often recoils on the head of the thrower.

Elizabeth I

One man with a head on his shoulders is worth a dozen without.

Elizabeth I

I would rather be a beggar and single than a queen and married.

Elizabeth I

I will make you shorter by the head.

Elizabeth I

Perfection is such a nuisance that I often regret having cured myself of using tobacco.

Emile Zola

He is a drunkard who takes more than three glasses though he be not drunk.

Epictetus

Neither should a ship rely on one small anchor, nor should life rest on a single hope.

Epictetus

When people complain of life, it is almost always because they have asked impossible things of it.

Ernest Renan

Virtue often trips and falls on the sharp-edges rock of poverty.

Eugene Sue

I am ashamed of confessing that I have nothing to confess.

Fanny Burney

It may seem a strange principle to enunciate as the very first requirement in a hospital that it should do the sick no harm.

Florence Nightingale

A bachelor's life is a fine breakfast, a flat lunch, and a miserable dinner.

Francis Bacon

Hope is a good breakfast, but it is a bad supper.

Francis Bacon

I will never be an old man. To me, old age is always 15 years older than I am.

Francis Bacon

It is impossible to love and to be wise.

Francis Bacon

Money is like manure, of very little use except it be spread.

Francis Bacon

Opportunity makes a thief.

Francis Bacon

People have discovered that they can fool the devil; but they can't fool the neighbors.

Francis Bacon

Rebellions of the belly are the worst.

Francis Bacon

The worst men often give the best advice.

Francis Bacon

The worst solitude is to have no real friendships.

Francis Bacon

Promises that you make to yourself are often like the Japanese plum tree - they bear no fruit.

Francis Marion

No man should have a political office because he wants a job.

Franklin Knight Lane

Frequently the more trifling the subject, the more animated and protracted the discussion.

Franklin Pierce

If my soldiers were to begin to think, not one of them would remain in the army.

Frederick II

I begin by taking. I shall find scholars later to demonstrate my perfect right.

Frederick II

As savage as a bear with a sore head.

Frederick Marryat

It's just six of one and half-a-dozen of the other.

Frederick Marryat

A casual stroll through the lunatic asylum shows that faith does not prove anything.

Friedrich Nietzsche

A pair of powerful spectacles has sometimes sufficed to cure a person in love.

Friedrich Nietzsche

A subject for a great poet would be God's boredom after the seventh day of creation.

Friedrich Nietzsche

A woman may very well form a friendship with a man, but for this to endure, it must be assisted by a little physical antipathy.

Friedrich Nietzsche

After coming into contact with a religious man I always feel I must wash my hands.

Friedrich Nietzsche

Ah, women. They make the highs higher and the lows more frequent.

Friedrich Nietzsche

All truth is simple... is that not doubly a lie?

Friedrich Nietzsche

Behind all their personal vanity, women themselves always have an impersonal contempt for woman.

Friedrich Nietzsche

Blessed are the forgetful: for they get the better even of their blunders.

Friedrich Nietzsche

Character is determined more by the lack of certain experiences than by those one has had.

Friedrich Nietzsche

Faith: not wanting to know what is true.

Friedrich Nietzsche

He who laughs best today, will also laughs last.

Friedrich Nietzsche

Idleness is the parent of psychology.

Friedrich Nietzsche

In heaven, all the interesting people are missing.

Friedrich Nietzsche

In individuals, insanity is rare; but in groups, parties, nations and epochs, it is the rule.

Friedrich Nietzsche

Is life not a thousand times too short for us to bore ourselves?

Friedrich Nietzsche

It is impossible to suffer without making someone pay for it; every complaint already contains revenge.

Friedrich Nietzsche

It is my ambition to say in ten sentences what others say in a whole book.

Friedrich Nietzsche

Many a man fails as an original thinker simply because his memory it too good.

Friedrich Nietzsche

One may sometimes tell a lie, but the grimace that accompanies it tells the truth.

Friedrich Nietzsche

The abdomen is the reason why man does not readily take himself to be a god.

Friedrich Nietzsche

The lie is a condition of life.

Friedrich Nietzsche

The most common lie is that which one lies to himself; lying to others is relatively an exception.

Friedrich Nietzsche

There cannot be a God because if there were one, I could not believe that I was not He.

Friedrich Nietzsche

There is more wisdom in your body than in your deepest philosophy.

Friedrich Nietzsche

To forget one's purpose is the commonest form of stupidity.

Friedrich Nietzsche

We hear only those questions for which we are in a position to find answers.

Friedrich Nietzsche

Whenever I climb I am followed by a dog called 'Ego'.

Friedrich Nietzsche

Wit is the epitaph of an emotion.

Friedrich Nietzsche

Woman was God's second mistake.

Friedrich Nietzsche

If there is no God, everything is permitted.

Fyodor Dostoevsky

Deprived of meaningful work, men and women lose their reason for existence; they go stark, raving mad.

Fyodor Dostoevsky

It is not possible to eat me without insisting that I sing praises of my devourer?

Fyodor Dostoevsky

The cleverest of all, in my opinion, is the man who calls himself a fool at least once a month.

Fyodor Dostoevsky

The formula 'Two and two make five' is not without its attractions.

Fyodor Dostoevsky

I'm not ugly, but my beauty is a total creation.

Georg Wilhelm Friedrich Hegel

Only one man ever understood me, and he didn't understand me.

Georg Wilhelm Friedrich Hegel

By common consent gray hairs are a crown of glory

George Bancroft

In nine times out of ten, the slanderous tongue belongs to a disappointed person.

George Bancroft

The public is wiser than the wisest critic.

George Bancroft

He who says there is no such thing as an honest man, you may be sure is himself a knave.

George Berkeley

I had rather be an oyster than a man, the most stupid and senseless of animals.

George Berkeley

The same principles which at first view lead to skepticism, pursued to a certain point, bring men back to common sense.

George Berkeley

Truth is the cry of all, but the game of few.

George Berkeley

We have first raised a dust and then complain we cannot see.

George Berkeley

Flippancy, the most hopeless form of intellectual vice.

George Gissing

It is because nations tend towards stupidity and baseness that mankind moves so slowly; it is because individuals have a capacity for better things that it moves at all.

George Gissing

Money is time. With money I buy for cheerful use the hours which otherwise would not in any sense be mine; nay, which would make me their miserable bondsman.

George Gissing

That is one of the bitter curses of poverty; it leaves no right to be generous.

George Gissing

Sometime I wish the aliens would abduct me and crown me as their leader.

George H. Walker

A traitor is everyone who does not agree with me.

George III

The human brain is a wonderful organ. It starts to work as soon as you are born and doesn't stop until you get up to deliver a speech.

George Jessel

A beast does not know that he is a beast, and the nearer a man gets to being a beast, the less he knows it.

George Macdonald

You can't live on amusement. It is the froth on water - an inch deep and then the mud.

George Macdonald

Caricature is rough truth.

George Meredith

I expect Woman will be the last thing civilized by Man.

George Meredith

Kissing don't last: cookery do!

George Meredith

She poured a little social sewage into his ears.

George Meredith

I have no enthusiasm for nature which the slightest chill will not instantly destroy.

George Sand

The best Qualification of a Prophet is to have a good Memory.

George Savile

Nothing has an uglier look to us than reason, when it is not on our side

George Savile

Most men make little use of their speech than to give evidence against their own understanding.

George Savile

Many men swallow the being cheated, but no man can ever endure to chew it.

George Savile

If the laws could speak for themselves, they would complain of the lawyers.

George Savile

Men's fame is like their hair, which grows after they are dead, and with just as little use to them.

George Villiers

With luck on your side, you can do without brains

Giordano Bruno

I would rather the man who presents something for my consideration subject me to a zephyr of truth and a gentle breeze of responsibility rather than blow me down with a curtain of hot wind.

Grover Cleveland

When man wanted to make a machine that would walk he created the wheel, which does not resemble a leg.

Guillaume Apollinaire

A superhuman will is needed in order to write, and I am only a man.

Gustave Flaubert

Anything becomes interesting if you look at it long enough.

Gustave Flaubert

Happiness is a monstrosity! Punished are those who seek it.

Gustave Flaubert

I love good sense above all, perhaps because I have none.

Gustave Flaubert

Nothing is more humiliating than to see idiots succeed in enterprises we have failed in.

Gustave Flaubert

The heart, like the stomach, wants a varied diet.

Gustave Flaubert

Writing is a dog's life, but the only life worth living.

Gustave Flaubert

If at first you do succeed - try to hide your astonishment.

Harry Banks

A little inaccuracy sometimes saves a ton of explanation.

Hector Hugh Munro

Addresses are given to us to conceal our whereabouts.

Hector Hugh Munro

Great Socialist statesmen aren't made, they're still-born.

Hector Hugh Munro

He's simply got the instinct for being unhappy highly developed.

Hector Hugh Munro

I always say beauty is only sin deep.

Hector Hugh Munro

It's no use growing older if you only learn new ways of misbehaving yourself.

Hector Hugh Munro

The young have aspirations that never come to pass, the old have reminiscences of what never happened.

Hector Hugh Munro

Common sense is calculation applied to life.

Henri Frederic Amiel

Destiny has two ways of crushing us - by refusing our wishes and by fulfilling them.

Henri Frederic Amiel

No man likes to have his intelligence or good faith questioned, especially if he has doubts about it himself.

Henry B. Adams

There is no such thing as an underestimate of average intelligence.

Henry B. Adams

Young men have a passion for regarding their elders as senile.

Henry B. Adams

Every generation laughs at the old fashions, but follows religiously the new.

Henry David Thoreau

A newspaper consists of just the same number of words, whether there be any news in it or not.

Henry Fielding

Commend a fool for his wit, or a rogue for his honesty and he will receive you into his favor.

Henry Fielding

Guilt has very quick ears to an accusation.

Henry Fielding

Money is the fruit of evil, as often as the root of it.

Henry Fielding

Neither great poverty nor great riches will hear reason.

Henry Fielding

One fool at least in every married couple.

Henry Fielding

When children are doing nothing, they are doing mischief. When I'm not thanked at all, I'm thanked enough, I've done my duty, and I've done no more.

Henry Fielding

Wine is a turncoat; first a friend and then an enemy.

Henry Fielding

How many men are there who fairly earn a million dollars?

Henry George

A careful driver is one who honks his horn when he goes through a red light.

Henry Morgan

People with insufficient personalities are fond of cats. These people adore being ignored.

Henry Morgan

Don't let your studies interfere with your education.

Henry Rutgers

On an exhausted field, only weeds grow.

Henry Sienkiewicz

The difference between perseverance and obstinacy is that one comes from a strong will, and the other from a strong won't.

Henry Ward Beecher

Success is full of promise till one gets it, and then it seems like a nest from which the bird has flown.

Henry Ward Beecher

Age and youth look upon life from the opposite ends of the telescope; it is exceedingly long, - it is exceedingly short

Henry Ward Beecher

Hide our ignorance as we will, an evening of wine soon reveals it.

Heraclitus

The chain of wedlock is so heavy that it takes two to carry it - and sometimes three.

Heraclitus

Our lives are universally shortened by our ignorance.

Herbert Spencer

Marriage: A word which should be pronounced "mirage".

Herbert Spencer

How often misused words generate misleading thoughts.

Herbert Spencer

A jury is composed of twelve men of average ignorance.

Herbert Spencer

A man thinks that by mouthing hard words he understands hard things.

Herman Melville

A smile is the chosen vehicle of all ambiguities.

Herman Melville

Better sleep with a sober cannibal than a drunken Christian.

Herman Melville

I am, as I am; whether hideous, or handsome, depends upon who is made judge.

Herman Melville

There are hardly five critics in America; and several of them are asleep.

Herman Melville

There is all of the difference in the world between paying and being paid.

Herman Melville

They talk of the dignity of work. The dignity is in leisure.

Herman Melville

To be called one thing, is oftentimes to be another.

Herman Melville

To be hated cordially, is only a left-handed compliment.

Herman Melville

To the last, I grapple with thee; From Hell's heart, I stab at thee; For hate's sake, I spit my last breath at thee.

Herman Melville

Truth is in things, and not in words.

Herman Melville

Death is a delightful hiding place for weary men.

Herodotus

It is easy to sit up and take notice, What is difficult is getting up and taking action.

Honore de Balzac

A flow of words is a sure sign of duplicity.

Honore de Balzac

A good marriage would be between a blind wife and a deaf husband.

Honore de Balzac

A husband who submits to his wife's yoke is justly held an object of ridicule. A woman's influence ought to be entirely concealed.

Honore de Balzac

A lover always thinks of his mistress first and himself second; with a husband it runs the other way.

Honore de Balzac

A man is a poor creature compared to a woman.

Honore de Balzac

A young bride is like a plucked flower; but a guilty wife is like a flower that had been walked over.

Honore de Balzac

Behind every great fortune lies a great crime.

Honore de Balzac

Bureaucracy is a giant mechanism operated by pygmies.

Honore de Balzac

Finance, like time, devours its own children.

Honore de Balzac

I do not regard a broker as a member of the human race.

Honore de Balzac

If we could but paint with the hand what we see with the eye.

Honore de Balzac

In diving to the bottom of pleasure we bring up more gravel than pearls.

Honore de Balzac

Laws are spider webs through which the big flies pass and the little ones get caught.

Honore de Balzac

Manners are the hypocrisy of a nation.

Honore de Balzac

Nature makes only dumb animals. We owe the fools to society.

Honore de Balzac

No man should marry until he has studied anatomy and dissected at least one woman.

Honore de Balzac

Solitude is fine, but you need someone to tell you that solitude is fine.

Honore de Balzac

The majority of husbands remind me of an orangutan trying to play the violin.

Honore de Balzac

The man as he converses is the lover; silent, he is the husband.

Honore de Balzac

There are some women whose pregnancy would make some sly bachelor smile.

Honore de Balzac

Be moderate in everything, including moderation.

Horace Porter

A mugwump is a person educated beyond his intellect.

Horace Porter

I have only one eye, I have a right to be blind sometimes... I really do not see the signal!

Horatio Nelson

Experience without theory is blind, but theory without experience is mere intellectual play.

Immanuel Kant

From such crooked wood as that which man is made of, nothing straight can be fashioned

Immanuel Kant

I had therefore to remove knowledge, in order to make room for belief.

Immanuel Kant

If man makes himself a worm he must not complain when he is trodden on.

Immanuel Kant

Acquaint yourself with your own ignorance.

Isaac Watts

It is a trick among the dishonest to offer sacrifices that are not needed, or not possible, to avoid making those that are required.

Ivan Goncharov

I agree with no one's opinion. I have some of my own.

Ivan Turgenev

Most people can't understand how others can blow their noses differently than they do.

Ivan Turgenev

The word tomorrow was invented for indecisive people and for children.

Ivan Turgenev

Women... can't live with 'em... can't shoot 'em.

Ivan Turgenev

A man always has two reasons for doing anything: a good reason and the real reason.

J.P. Morgan

If you have to ask how much it costs, you can't afford it.

J.P. Morgan

A bone to the dog is not charity. Charity is the bone shared with the dog, when you are just as hungry as the dog.

Jack London

I would rather be a superb meteor, every atom of me in magnificent glow, than a sleepy and permanent planet.

Jack London

If cash comes with fame, come fame; if cash comes without fame, come cash.

Jack London

Life is not a matter of holding good cards, but sometimes, playing a poor hand well.

Jack London

You can't wait for inspiration. You have to go after it with a club.

Jack London

It was hard to make fun of him because he seemed to have so much fun making fun of himself.

James Barron

He who has provoked the lash of wit, cannot complain that he smarts from it.

James Boswell

I hate mankind, for I think myself one of the best of them, and I know how bad I am.

James Boswell

I have found you an argument; I am not obliged to find you an understanding.

James Boswell

What an insignificant life is this which I am now leading!

James Boswell

Man cannot live by bread alone; he must have peanut butter.

James Garfield

The truth will set you free, but first it will make you miserable.

James Garfield

Men are never so good or so bad as their opinions.

James Mackintosh

Philosophy is common sense with big words.

James Madison

Tell me what you eat and I'll tell you who you are.

Jean Anthelme Brillat-Savarin

The discovery of a new dish confers more happiness on humanity, than the discovery of a new star.

Jean Anthelme Brillat-Savarin

A man can keep another's secret better than his own. A woman her own better than others.

Jean de la Bruyere

A mediocre mind thinks it writes divinely; a good mind thinks it writes reasonably.

Jean de la Bruyere

If some persons died, and others did not die, death would be a terrible affliction.

Jean de la Bruyere

It is a sad thing when men have neither the wit to speak well nor the judgment to hold their tongues.

Jean de la Bruyere

Men blush less for their crimes than for their weaknesses and vanity.

Jean de la Bruyere

Next to sound judgment, diamonds and pearls are the rarest things in the world.

Jean de la Bruyere

One mark of a second-rate mind is to be always telling stories.

Jean de la Bruyere

One must laugh before one is happy, or one may die without ever laughing at all.

Jean de la Bruyere

One seeks to make the loved one entirely happy, or, if that cannot be, entirely wretched.

Jean de la Bruyere

Poverty may be the mother of crime, but lack of good sense is the father.

Jean de la Bruyere

The wise person often shuns society for fear of being bored.

Jean de la Bruyere

Those who make the worst use of their time are the first to complain of its brevity.

Jean de la Bruyere

Age doesn't matter, unless your cheese.

Jean Paul

Plant and your spouse plants with you; weed and you weed alone.

Jean-Jacques Rousseau

How many famous and high-spirited heroes have lived a day too long?

Jean-Jacques Rousseau

Lawyers are the only persons in whom ignorance of the law is not punished.

Jeremy Bentham

The power of the lawyer is in the uncertainty of the law.

Jeremy Bentham

Trust him not with your secrets, who, when left alone in your room, turns over your papers.

Johann Kaspar Lavater

There are three classes of men; the retrograde, the stationary and the progressive.

Johann Kaspar Lavater

The jealous are possessed by a mad devil and a dull spirit at the same time.

Johann Kaspar Lavater

Him, who incessantly laughs in the street, you may commonly hear grumbling in his closet.

Johann Kaspar Lavater

Like blind hens, we are ignorant of our own self and the depths within us.

Johannes Tauler

A good idea plus capable men cannot fail; it is better than money in the bank.

John Berry

Popular applause veers with the wind.

John Bright

I consider looseness with words no less of a defect than looseness of the bowels.

John Calvin

It is easier for a tutor to command than to teach.

John Locke

All thing I thought I knew; but now confess, the more I know I know, I know the less.

John Owen

In this administration, a place can be found for every bad man.

John Philpot Curran

His smile is like the silver plate on a coffin.

John Philpot Curran

Although it is not true that all conservatives are stupid people, it is true that most stupid people are conservative.

John Stuart Mill

He who knows only his own side of the case knows little of that.

John Stuart Mill

In all intellectual debates, both sides tend to be correct in what they affirm, and wrong in what they deny.

John Stuart Mill

That so few now dare to be eccentric, marks the chief danger of the time.

John Stuart Mill

The despotism of custom is everywhere the standing hindrance to human advancement.

John Stuart Mill

Zeal is fit for wise men, but flourishes chiefly among fools.

John Tillotson

Courtesies cannot be borrowed like snow shovels; you must have some of your own.

John Wanamaker

Half the money I spend on advertising is wasted; the trouble is, I don't know which half.

John Wanamaker

It's easy to work for somebody else; all you have to do is show up.

John Wanamaker

No wise man ever wished to be younger.

Jonathan Swift

Promises and pie-crust are made to be broken.

Jonathan Swift

Others go to bed with their mistresses; I with my ideas.

Jose Marti

You cannot teach old dogs new tricks.

Joseph Chamberlain

I don't know what a scoundrel is like, but I know what a respectable man is like, and it's enough to make one's flesh creep.

Joseph De Maistre

There is no philosophy without the art of ignoring objections.

Joseph De Maistre

If hard work were such a wonderful thing, surely the rich would have kept it all to themselves.

Joseph Kirkland

A dog is the only thing on earth that loves you more than you love yourself.

Josh Billings

About the most originality that any writer can hope to achieve honestly is to steal with good judgment.

Josh Billings

About the only difference between the poor and the rich, is this, the poor suffer misery, while the rich have to enjoy it.

Josh Billings

Advice is like castor oil, easy enough to give but dreadful uneasy to take.

Josh Billings

Confess your sins to the Lord and you will be forgiven; confess them to man and you will be laughed at.

Josh Billings

Flattery is like cologne water, to be smelt, not swallowed.

Josh Billings

I have never known a person to live to be one hundred and be remarkable for anything else.

Josh Billings

It ain't often that a man's reputation outlasts his money.

Josh Billings

Money will buy a pretty good dog, but it won't buy the wag of his tail.

Josh Billings

The best way to convince a fool that he is wrong is to let him have his own way.

Josh Billings

There are lots of people who mistake their imagination for their memory.

Josh Billings

Let me say no danger and no hardship ever makes me wish to get back to that college life again.

Joshua Chamberlain

Capital is dead labor, which, vampire-like, lives only by sucking living labor, and lives the more, the more labor it sucks.

Karl Marx

History repeats itself, first as tragedy, second as farce.

Karl Marx

I am not a Marxist.

Karl Marx

Machines were, it may be said, the weapon employed by the capitalists to quell the revolt of specialized labor.

Karl Marx

Sell a man a fish, he eats for a day, teach a man how to fish, you ruin a wonderful business opportunity.

Karl Marx

The only antidote to mental suffering is physical pain.

Karl Marx

The rich will do anything for the poor but get off their backs.

Karl Marx

While the miser is merely a capitalist gone mad, the capitalist is a rational miser.

Karl Marx

Now that I am a deputy, I will cease to be an agitator.

Lajos Kossuth

Those who have knowledge, don't predict. Those who predict, don't have knowledge.

Lao Tzu

If you do not change direction, you may end up where you are heading.

Lao Tzu

He who talks more is sooner exhausted.

Lao Tzu

Born to be wild - live to outgrow it.

Lao Tzu

An ant on the move does more than a dozing ox.

Lao Tzu

For every ten jokes you acquire a hundred enemies.

Laurence Sterne

Men tire themselves in the pursuit of sleep.

Laurence Sterne

Nothing is so perfectly amusing as a total change of ideas.

Laurence Sterne

He never chooses an opinion; he just wears whatever happens to be in style.

Leo Tolstoy

Historians are like deaf people who go on answering questions that no one has asked them.

Leo Tolstoy

A proverb is the wisdom of many and the wit of one.

Lord Russell

It is legal because I wish it.

Louis XIV

I could sooner reconcile all Europe than two women.

Louis XIV

Every time I create an appointment, I create a hundred malcontents and one ingrate.

Louis XIV

Father asked us what was God's noblest work. Anna said men, but I said babies. Men are often bad, but babies never are.

Louisa May Alcott

Girls are so queer you never know what they mean. They say No when they mean Yes, and drive a man out of his wits for the fun of it.

Louisa May Alcott

Housekeeping ain't no joke.

Louisa May Alcott

People don't have fortunes left them in that style nowadays; men have to work and women to marry for money. It's a dreadfully unjust world.

Louisa May Alcott

Resolve to take fate by the throat and shake a living out of her.

Louisa May Alcott

Money is the root of all evil, and yet it is such a useful root that we cannot get on without it any more than we can without potatoes

Louisa May Alcott

It is difficult to esteem a man as highly as he would wish.

Luc de Clapiers

Obscurity is the realm of error.

Luc de Clapiers

The fool is like those people who think themselves rich with little.

Luc de Clapiers

Do not consider it proof just because it is written in books, for a liar who will deceive with his tongue will not hesitate to do the same with his pen.

Maimonides

No disease that can be treated by diet should be treated with any other means.

Maimonides

You must become an old man in good time if you wish to be an old man long.

Marcus Aurelius

To the wise, life is a problem; to the fool, a solution.

Marcus Aurelius

The object in life is not to be on the side of the majority, but to escape finding oneself in the ranks of the insane.

Marcus Aurelius

The art of living is more like wrestling than dancing.

Marcus Aurelius

How much time he saves who does not look to see what his neighbor says or does or thinks.

Marcus Aurelius

How much more grievous are the consequences of anger than the causes of it.

Marcus Aurelius

Because a thing seems difficult for you, do not think it impossible for anyone to accomplish.

Marcus Aurelius

Fortune's wheel never stands still the highest point is therefore the most perilous

Maria Edgeworth

An orator is the worse person to tell a plain fact.

Maria Edgeworth

How success changes the opinion of men!

Maria Edgeworth

I've a great fancy to see my own funeral afore I die.

Maria Edgeworth

There is nothing new except what has been forgotten.

Marie Antoinette

I have seen all, I have heard all, I have forgotten all.

Marie Antoinette

Even a stopped clock is right twice a day.

Marie von Ebner-Eschenbach

If you have one good idea, people will lend you twenty.

Marie von Ebner-Eschenbach

Nobody knows enough, but many know too much.

Marie von Ebner-Eschenbach

None are so eager to gain new experience as those who don't know how to make use of the old ones.

Marie von Ebner-Eschenbach

Parents forgive their children least readily for the faults they themselves instilled in them.

Marie von Ebner-Eschenbach

Those who understand only what can be explained understand very little.

Marie von Ebner-Eschenbach

To be content with little is hard; to be content with much, impossible.

Marie von Ebner-Eschenbach

We are so vain that we even care for the opinion of those we don't care for

Marie von Ebner-Eschenbach

We don't believe in rheumatism and true love until after the first attack.

Marie von Ebner-Eschenbach

Wrinkles should merely indicate where smiles have been.

Mark Twain

Don't go around saying the world owes you a living. The world owes you nothing. It was here first

Mark Twain

Age is an issue of mind over matter. If you don't mind, it doesn't matter.

Mark Twain

It is not best that we should all think alike; it is a difference of opinion that makes horse races.

Mark Twain

A banker is a fellow who lends you his umbrella when the sun is shining, but wants it back the minute it begins to rain.

Mark Twain

I was gratified to be able to answer promptly, and I did. I said I didn't know. A lie can travel half way around the world while the truth is putting on its shoes.

Mark Twain

Name the greatest of all inventors. Accident.

Mark Twain

The difference between the right word and almost the right word is the difference between lightning and the lightning bug.

Mark Twain

Truth titillates the imagination far less than fiction.

Marquis de Sade

Give the lady what she wants!

Marshall Field

I live a very dull life here... indeed I think I am more like a state prisoner than anything else.

Martha Washington

Be thou comforted, little dog, Thou too in Resurrection shall have a little golden tail.

Martin Luther

I feel much freer now that I am certain the pope is the Antichrist.

Martin Luther

If I am not allowed to laugh in heaven, I don't want to go there.

Martin Luther

Reason is a whore, the greatest enemy that faith has.

Martin Luther

My evil genius Procrastination has whispered me to tarry 'til a more convenient season.

Mary Todd Lincoln

A good marriage would be between a blind wife and a deaf husband.

Michel de Montaigne

Age imprints more wrinkles in the mind than it does on the face. An untempted woman cannot boast of her chastity.

Michel de Montaigne

Death, they say, acquits us of all obligations.

Michel de Montaigne

Every one rushes elsewhere and into the future, because no one wants to face one's own inner self.

Michel de Montaigne

Fortune, seeing that she could not make fools wise, has made them lucky.

Michel de Montaigne

He who establishes his argument by noise and command shows that his reason is weak.

Michel de Montaigne

How many things we held yesterday as articles of faith which today we tell as fables.

Michel de Montaigne

I do not speak the minds of others except to speak my own mind better.

Michel de Montaigne

I have never seen a greater monster or miracle in the world than myself.

Michel de Montaigne

I know well what I am fleeing from but not what I am in search of.

Michel de Montaigne

I quote others only in order the better to express myself.

Michel de Montaigne

If ordinary people complain that I speak too much of myself, I complain that they do not even think of themselves.

Michel de Montaigne

If there is such a thing as a good marriage, it is because it resembles friendship rather than love.

Michel de Montaigne

Ignorance is the softest pillow on which a man can rest his head.

Michel de Montaigne

In nine lifetimes, you'll never know as much about your cat as your cat knows about you.

Michel de Montaigne

Marriage is like a cage; one sees the birds outside desperate to get in, and those inside equally desperate to get out.

Michel de Montaigne

Marriage, a market which has nothing free but the entrance.

Michel de Montaigne

Stubborn and ardent clinging to one's opinion is the best proof of stupidity.

Michel de Montaigne

The way of the world is to make laws, but follow custom.

Michel de Montaigne

The world is but a perpetual see-saw.

Michel de Montaigne

There is no conversation more boring than the one where everybody agrees.

Michel de Montaigne

Unless a man feels he has a good enough memory, he should never venture to lie.

Michel de Montaigne

When I play with my cat, who knows whether she is not amusing herself with me more than I with her.

Michel de Montaigne

Wit is a dangerous weapon, even to the possessor, if he knows not how to use it discreetly.

Michel de Montaigne

A closed mouth catches no flies.

Miguel de Cervantes

A proverb is a short sentence based on long experience.

Miguel de Cervantes

Drink moderately, for drunkeness neither keeps a secret, nor observes a promise.

Miguel de Cervantes

God bears with the wicked, but not forever.

Miguel de Cervantes

Doing good to base fellows is like throwing water into the sea.

Miguel de Cervantes

Laziness never arrived at the attainment of a good wish.

Miguel de Cervantes

Man appoints, and God disappoints.

Miguel de Cervantes

No fathers or mothers think their own children ugly.

Miguel de Cervantes

No padlocks, bolts, or bars can secure a maiden better than her own reserve.

Miguel de Cervantes

That which costs little is less valued.

Miguel de Cervantes

That's the nature of women, not to love when we love them, and to love when we love them not.

Miguel de Cervantes

There's no taking trout with dry breeches.

Miguel de Cervantes

Those who'll play with cats must expect to be scratched.

Miguel de Cervantes

A Constitution should be short and obscure.

Napolean Bonaparte

A man will fight harder for his interests than for his rights.

Napolean Bonaparte

A throne is only a bench covered with velvet.

Napolean Bonaparte

Doctors will have more lives to answer for in the next world than even we generals.

Napolean Bonaparte

He who knows how to flatter also knows how to slander.

Napolean Bonaparte

History is a set of lies agreed upon.

Napolean Bonaparte

If they want peace, nations should avoid the pin-pricks that precede cannon shots.

Napolean Bonaparte

If you wish to be a success in the world, promise everything, deliver nothing.

Napolean Bonaparte

Impossible is a word to be found only in the dictionary of fools.

Napolean Bonaparte

In politics stupidity is not a handicap.

Napolean Bonaparte

Never interrupt your enemy when he is making a mistake.

Napolean Bonaparte

Power is my mistress. I have worked too hard at her conquest to allow anyone to take her away from me.

Napolean Bonaparte

Religion is excellent stuff for keeping common people quiet.

Napolean Bonaparte

The best way to keep one's word is not to give it.

Napolean Bonaparte

The French complain of everything, and always.

Napolean Bonaparte

The great proof of madness is the disproportion of one's designs to one's means.

Napolean Bonaparte

The surest way to remain poor is to be an honest man.

Napolean Bonaparte

There is only one step from the sublime to the ridiculous.

Napolean Bonaparte

Throw off your worries when you throw off your clothes at night.

Napolean Bonaparte

We must laugh at man to avoid crying for him.

Napolean Bonaparte

No damn man kills me and lives.

Nathan Bedford Forrest

A woman's chastity consists, like an onion, of a series of coats.

Nathaniel Hawthorne

Easy reading is damn hard writing.

Nathaniel Hawthorne

What other dungeon is so dark as one's own heart! What jailer so inexorable as one's self!

Nathaniel Hawthorne

Prejudices are not easily got rid of as an old coat which is no longer thought of.

Nicholas Malebranche

You find yourself in the world, without any power, immovable as a rock, stupid, so to speak, as a log of wood.

Nicholas Malebranche

Put your trust in God; but be sure to keep your powder dry.

Oliver Cromwell

Do not trust the cheering, for those persons would shout as much if you or I were going to be hanged.

Oliver Cromwell

A journalist is a person who has mistaken their calling.

Otto von Bismarck

I have seen three emperors in their nakedness, and the sight was not inspiring.

Otto von Bismarck

Laws are like sausages, it is better not to see them being made.

Otto von Bismarck

Never believe anything in politics until it has been officially denied.

Otto von Bismarck

People never lie so much as after a hunt, during a war or before an election.

Otto von Bismarck

Politics is the art of the next best.

Otto von Bismarck

Politics ruins the character.

Otto von Bismarck

When a man says that he approves something in principal, it means he hasn't the slightest intention of putting it in practice.

Otto von Bismarck

When you want to fool the world, tell the truth.

Otto von Bismarck

A cruel story runs on wheels, and every hand oils the wheels as they run.

Ouida

An easy-going husband is the one indispensable comfort of life.

Ouida

Familiarity is a magician that is cruel to beauty but kind to ugliness.

Ouida

Petty laws breed great crimes.

Ouida

To vice, innocence must always seem only a superior kind of chicanery.

Ouida

The truth only irritates those it enlightens, but does not convert.

Paquier Quesnel

If this be treason, make the most of it!

Patrick Henry

Love without sex is still the most efficient form of hell known to man.

Peter Porter

I know too much to be a sceptic and too little to be a dogmatist.

Pierre Bayle

The easiest way to be cheated is to believe yourself to be more cunning than others.

Pierre Charron

Opinion is the medium between knowledge and ignorance.

Plato

Attention to health is life greatest hindrance.

Plato

Cunning... is but the low mimic of wisdom.

Plato

He was a wise man who invented beer.

Plato

He who steals a little steals with the same wish as he who steals much, but with less power.

Plato

Honesty is for the most part less profitable than dishonesty.

Plato

I have hardly ever known a mathematician who was capable of reasoning.

Plato

Love is a serious mental disease.

Plato

Nothing in the affairs of men is worthy of great anxiety.

Plato

Opinion is the medium between knowledge and ignorance.

Plato

The heaviest penalty for deciding to engage in politics is to be ruled by someone inferior to yourself.

Plato

There are three classes of men; lovers of wisdom, lovers of honor, and lovers of gain.

Plato

They do certainly give very strange, and newfangled, names to diseases.

Plato

Those who are too smart to engage in politics are punished by being governed by those who are dumber.

Plato

Wealth is well known to be a great comforter.

Plato

Mankind is poised midway between the gods and the beasts.

Plotinus

I feel sure that no girl would go to the altar if she knew all

Queen Victoria

I don't dislike babies, though I think very young ones rather disgusting.

Queen Victoria

Being pregnant is an occupational hazard of being a wife.

Queen Victoria

A marriage is no amusement but a solemn act, and generally a sad one.

Queen Victoria

Those who wish to appear wise among fools, among the wise seem foolish.

Quintilian

Avoid any specific discussion of public policy at public meetings.

Quintus Tullius Cicero

For every minute you remain angry, you give up sixty seconds of peace of mind.

Ralph Waldo Emerson

If you want to go east, don't go west.

Ramakrishna

The fabled musk deer searches the world over for the source of the scent which comes from itself.

Ramakrishna

When the flower blooms, the bees come uninvited.

Ramakrishna

Man has made use of his intelligence, he invented stupidity.

Remy de Gourmont

Of all the sexual aberrations, perhaps the most peculiar is chastity.

Remy de Gourmont

Simple ideas lie within the reach only of complex minds.

Remy de Gourmont

The terrible thing about the quest for truth is that you find it.

Remy de Gourmont

Thinking is hard work. One can't bear burdens and ideas at the same time.

Remy de Gourmont

People who eat potatoes will never be able to perform their abilities in whatever job they choose to have.

Richard Cobden

My organs are too powerful... I manufacture blood and fat too rapidly.

Robert Baldwin

He that said it was not good for man to be alone, placed the celibate amongst the inferior states of perfection.

Robert Boyle

Perhaps one has to be very old before one learns to be amused rather than shocked.

Robert Browning

It's wiser being good than bad; It's safer being meek than fierce: It's fitter being sane than mad.

Robert Browning

Whiskey - I like it, I always did, and that is the reason I never use it. The devil's name is dullness.

Robert E. Lee

The devil's name is dullness.

Robert E. Lee

Anger is a wind which blows out the lamp of the mind.

Robert Ingersoll

Hope is the only bee that makes honey without flowers.

Robert Ingersoll

If I owe Smith ten dollars and God forgives me, that doesn't pay Smith.

Robert Ingersoll

Ignorance is the soil in which belief in miracles grows.

Robert Ingersoll

It is an old habit with theologians to beat the living with the bones of the dead.

Robert Ingersoll

There seem to me to be very few facts, at least ascertainable facts, in politics.

Robert Peel

Better be killed than frightened to death.

Robert Smith Surtee

Hang 'em first, try 'em later.

Roy Bean

I know the law... I am it's greatest transgressor.

Roy Bean

You have been tried by twelve good men and true, not of your peers but as high above you as heaven is of hell, and they have said you are guilty.

Roy Bean

The truth is, this being errand boy to one hundred and fifty thousand people tires me so by night I am ready for bed instead of soirees.

Rutherford B. Hayes

To many, total abstinence is easier than perfect moderation.

Saint Augustine

Give me chastity and continence, but not quite yet.

Saint Augustine

If God can work through me, he can work through anyone.

Saint Francis of Assisi

Marriage is good for those who are afraid to sleep alone at night.

Saint Jerome

Keep doing some kind of work, that the devil may always find you employed.

Saint Jerome

A fat stomach never breeds fine thoughts.

Saint Jerome

A beautiful woman must expect to be more accountable for her steps, than one less attractive.

Samuel Richardson

A husband's mother and his wife had generally better be visitors than inmates.

Samuel Richardson

A Stander-by is often a better judge of the game than those that play.

Samuel Richardson

Every scholar, I presume, is not, necessarily, a man of sense.

Samuel Richardson

Handsome husbands often make a wife's heart ache.

Samuel Richardson

It is better to be thought perverse than insincere.

Samuel Richardson

It is much easier to find fault with others, than to be faultless ourselves.

Samuel Richardson

Married people should not be quick to hear what is said by either when in ill humor.

Samuel Richardson

Men generally are afraid of a wife who has more understanding than themselves.

Samuel Richardson

Necessity may well be called the mother of invention but calamity is the test of integrity.

Samuel Richardson

People of little understanding are most apt to be angry when their sense is called into question.

Samuel Richardson

Shame is a fitter and generally a more effectual punishment for a child than beating.

Samuel Richardson

The companion of an evening, and the companion for life, require very different qualifications.

Samuel Richardson

There would be no supporting life were we to feel quite as poignantly for others as we do for ourselves.

Samuel Richardson

Those we dislike can do nothing to please us.

Samuel Richardson

Those who have least to do are generally the most busy people in the world.

Samuel Richardson

We are all very ready to believe what we like.

Samuel Richardson

Where words are restrained, the eyes often talk a great deal.

Samuel Richardson

Women do not often fall in love with philosophers.

Samuel Richardson

When I am in the cellar of affliction, I look for the Lord's choicest wines.

Samuel Rutherford

It is the part of a fool to say, I should not have thought.

Scipio Africanus

I'm never less at leisure than when at leisure, or less alone than when alone.

Scipio Africanus

I am convinced that life is 10% what happens to me and 96% how I react to it.

Scipio Africanus

Judgement comes from experience, and experience comes from bad judgement.

Simon Bolivar

Half the lies our opponents tell about us are untrue.

Sir Boyle Roche

Every pint bottle should contain a quart.

Sir Boyle Roche

Worthless people live only to eat and drink; people of worth eat and drink only to live.

Socrates

My advice to you is get married: if you find a good wife you'll be happy; if not, you'll become a philosopher.

Socrates

I was really too honest a man to be a politician and live.

Socrates

Beware the barrenness of a busy life.

Socrates

As to marriage or celibacy, let a man take which course he will, he will be sure to repent.

Socrates

It is so hard to believe because it is so hard to obey.

Soren Kierkegaard

Most men pursue pleasure with such breathless haste that they hurry past it.

Soren Kierkegaard

People demand freedom of speech as a compensation for the freedom of thought which they seldom use.

Soren Kierkegaard

Take away paradox from the thinker and you have a professor.

Soren Kierkegaard

I am more afraid of alcohol than of all the bullets of the enemy.

Stonewall Jackson

The skilful employer of men will employ the wise man, the brave man, the covetous man, and the stupid man.

Sun Tzu

If you could kick the person in the pants responsible for most of your trouble, you wouldn't sit for a month.

Theodore Roosevelt

I am only an average man but, by George, I work harder at it than the average man.

Theodore Roosevelt

The human body has two ends on it: one to create with and one to sit on. Sometimes people get their ends reversed. When this happens they need a kick in the seat of the pants.

Theodore Roosevelt

I keep my good health by having a very bad temper, kept under good control.

Theodore Roosevelt

I have only a second rate brain, but I think I have a capacity for action.

Theodore Roosevelt

The only man who never makes a mistake, is the man who never does anything.

Theodore Roosevelt

Sorrow can be alleviated by good sleep, a bath and a glass of wine.

Thomas Aquinas

If the highest aim of a captain were to preserve his ship, he would keep it in port forever.

Thomas Aquinas

A man without a goal is like a ship without a rudder.

Thomas Carlyle

A well-written life is almost as rare as a well-spent one.

Thomas Carlyle

I do not believe in the collective wisdom of individual ignorance.

Thomas Carlyle

I don't pretend to understand the Universe - it's a great deal bigger than I am.

Thomas Carlyle

Imagination is a poor matter when it has to part company with understanding.

Thomas Carlyle

It is a vain hope to make people happy by politics.

Thomas Carlyle

Love is not altogether a delirium, yet it has many points in common therewith.

Thomas Carlyle

Make yourself an honest man, and then you may be sure there is one less rascal in the world.

Thomas Carlyle

No person is important enough to make me angry.

Thomas Carlyle

No pressure, no diamonds.

Thomas Carlyle

Science must have originated in the feeling that something was wrong.

Thomas Carlyle

Teach a parrot the terms "supply and demand" and you've got an economist.

Thomas Carlyle

The real use of gunpowder is to make all men tall.

Thomas Carlyle

There are good and bad times, but our mood changes more often than our fortune.

Thomas Carlyle

Weak eyes are fondest of glittering objects.

Thomas Carlyle

What we become depends on what we read after all of the professors have finished with us.

Thomas Carlyle

A good garden may have some weeds.

Thomas Fuller

Get the facts, or the facts will get you. And when you get em, get em right, or they will get you wrong.

Thomas Fuller

A wise man should so write (though in words understood by all men) that wise men only should be able to commend him.

Thomas Hobbes

The condition of man... is a condition of war of everyone against everyone.

Thomas Hobbes

The privilege of absurdity; to which no living creature is subject, but man only.

Thomas Hobbes

I am more afraid of alcohol than of all the bullets of the enemy.

Thomas J. Jackson

Advertisements contain the only truths to be relied on in a newspaper.

Thomas Jefferson

Do not bite at the bait of pleasure, till you know there is no hook beneath it.

Thomas Jefferson

My only fear is that I may live too long. This would be a subject of dread to me.

Thomas Jefferson

We never repent of having eaten too little.

Thomas Jefferson

A writer may tell me that he thinks man will ultimately become an ostrich. I cannot properly contradict him.

Thomas Malthus

I know only two tunes: one of them is "Yankee Doodle," and the other isn't.

Ulysses S. Grant

True philosophy invents nothing; it merely establishes and describes what is.

Victor Cousin

You may not realize it when it happens, but a kick in the teeth may be the best thing in the world for you.

Walt Disney

Laughter is America's most important export.

Walt Disney

A rusty nail placed near a faithful compass, will sway it from the truth, and wreck the argosy.

Walter Scott

If you once turn on your side after the hour at which you ought to rise, it is all over. Bolt up at once.

Walter Scott

O, what a tangled web we weave when first we practise to deceive!

Walter Scott

Of all vices, drinking is the most incompatible with greatness.

Walter Scott

Whenever a man's friends begin to compliment him about looking young, he may be sure that they think he is growing old.

Washington Irving

A tart temper never mellows with age, and a sharp tongue is the only edged tool that grows keener with constant use.

Washington Irving

Agitation is the atmosphere of the brains

Wendell Phillips

Ambition may be defined as the willingness to receive any number of hits on the nose.

Wilfred Owen

I am not against hasty marriages where a mutual flame is fanned by an adequate income.

Wilkie Collins

The horrid mystery hanging over us in this house gets into my head like liquor, and makes me wild.

Wilkie Collins

The law will argue any thing, with any body who will pay the law for the use of its brains and its time.

Wilkie Collins

The profession of a prostitute is the only career in which the maximum income is paid to the newest apprentice.

William Booth

To be poor and independent is very nearly an impossibility

William Cobbett

I believe that economists put decimal points in their forecasts to show they have a sense of humor.

William Gilmore Simms

Billing and cooing to me is worse to witness an execution.

William Hamilton Maxwell

I am naturally taciturn, and became a silent and attentive listener.

William Hamilton Maxwell

To Englishmen, life is a topic, not an activity.

William Henry Harrison

The public be damned.

William Henry Vanderbilt

A great many people think they are thinking when they are merely rearranging their prejudices.

William James

Compared to what we ought to be, we are half awake.

William James

Everybody should do at least two things each day that he hates to do, just for practice.

William James

If merely 'feeling good' could decide, drunkenness would be the supremely valid human experience.

William James

Is life worth living? It all depends on the liver.

William James

It is our attitude at the beginning of a difficult task which, more than anything else, will affect its successful outcome.

William James

The aim of a college education is to teach you to know a good man when you see one.

William James

The art of being wise is the art of knowing what to overlook.

William James

The greatest weapon against stress is our ability to choose one thought over another.

William James

The world is all the richer for having a devil in it, so long as we keep our foot upon his neck.

William James

To be a real philosopher all that is necessary is to hate some one else's type of thinking.

William James

What I want is men who will support me when I am in the wrong.

William Lamb

A clever, ugly man every now and then is successful with the ladies, but a handsome fool is irresistible.

William Makepeace Thackeray

An evil person is like a dirty window, they never let the light shine through.

William Makepeace Thackeray

Dinner was made for eating, not for talking.

William Makepeace Thackeray

Except for the young or very happy, I can't say I am sorry for anyone who dies.

William Makepeace Thackeray

I never knew whether to pity or congratulate a man on coming to his senses.

William Makepeace Thackeray

It is impossible, in our condition of Society, not to be sometimes a Snob.

William Makepeace Thackeray

Next to the young, I suppose the very old are the most selfish.

William Makepeace Thackeray

People hate as they love, unreasonably.

William Makepeace Thackeray

'Tis strange what a man may do, and a woman yet think him an angel.

William Makepeace Thackeray

Avoid popularity; it has many snares, and no real benefit.

William Penn

Force may make hypocrites, but it can never make converts.

William Penn

Humility and knowledge in poor clothes excel pride and ignorance in costly attire.

William Penn

Men are generally more careful of the breed of their horses and dogs than of their children.

William Penn

The jealous are troublesome to others, but a torment to themselves.

William Penn

Poverty of course is no disgrace, but it is damned annoying.

William Pitt

Truth is not only stranger than fiction, it is more interesting.

William Randolph

The greatest right in the world is the right to be wrong.

William Randolph

A politician will do anything to keep his job - even become a patriot.

William Randolph

Whatever you have, spend less.

William Samuel Johnson

To keep your secret is wisdom; to expect others to keep it is folly.

William Samuel Johnson

You may as well say, 'That's a valiant flea that dare eat his breakfast on the lip of a lion.

William Tecumseh Sherman

War is the remedy that our enemies have chosen, and I say let us give them all they want.

William Tecumseh Sherman

I have often repented speaking, but never of holding my tongue.

Xenocrates

I once tried thinking for an entire day, but I found it less valuable than one moment of study.

Xun Zi

www.ingramcontent.com/pod-product-compliance
Lightning Source LLC
Chambersburg PA
CBHW082326290526
45793CB00009B/784